Fred

To one of my best

and favorite managers.

Dave G Stuie

6/2012

THE COACH

13 SKILLS TO ENHANCE YOUR CAREER

David G. Giese

Life and Business Coach

authorHOUSE®

AuthorHouse™
1663 Liberty Drive
Bloomington, IN 47403
www.authorhouse.com
Phone: 1-800-839-8640

Published by AuthorHouse 2/27/2012

ISBN: 978-1-4685-4806-8 (e)
ISBN: 978-1-4685-4807-5 (hc)
ISBN: 978-1-4685-4808-2 (sc)

Library of Congress Control Number: 2012901828

I dedicate this book to my oldest son, whom I love and am so very proud of. As he graduates from college this year, I know the skills explained in this book will help him with his upcoming transition.

Contents

Preface

After a college education in business management, thirty years of business experience at two outstanding companies (IBM and Dell) and many hours of mentoring my employees, colleagues and friends, I thought it best to capture the many messages I have shared with them over the years. These skills were gathered from my own personal education, experience and research. In communicating these thirteen skills, I hope to complement all the reader's current skill set and further enhance both their careers and personal lives.

The book shares an easy to use personal development process and the thirteen skills I believe anyone that works needs to know, internalize and practice. I leverage a dialogue between Kenneth, a business-savvy and wise mentor, and Cameron, the mentee, who is relatively new in his career to convey my messages. I hope and pray this book's contents will aid you no matter where you are in your career and life. Thank you for the opportunity to share my experiences with you and best of luck in the pursuit of your career goals and personal objectives.

David G. Giese

Acknowledgments

From the age of eighteen through today, I have studied many positive examples on the subject of personal development and success. The use of short sayings and quotes has been a simple yet useful tool to drive improvements for me. Through their seminars, books, audiotapes, and CDs, my mentors have taught me many lessons and provided me several quotes, some used in this book, and other thoughts for guidance that have not only helped me in my life but have allowed me to help others as well. If you are not already a student of theirs, I recommend you consider becoming one in the future.

I would like to thank and acknowledge them for their positive guidance:

The Bible

Stephen R. Covey

Wayne Dyer

Benjamin Franklin

Napoleon Hill

Tom Hopkins

Bob Moawad

Norman V. Peale

Jim Rohn

Brian Tracy

Denis Waitley

Zig Ziglar

Chapter 1

I Learned That Change Is Good

How fortunate I was when I landed a great job aligned with my education and interests upon graduating from school. Yet after only nine months with my company, I learned that only one thing in business was constant, and that was *change*. Though I had become more and more comfortable with my company, my manager, and my current responsibilities within my department, an organizational change occurred, placing me in basically the same job but in a new department with a different manager. My name is Cameron, and I look forward to sharing my notes with you on what I learned from the profound experience that I received as a result of that fortunate change.

During the first meeting with my new manager, I could tell that he had a different management style. He was not only focused on meeting the business results assigned to the department but was also equally concerned about his team and their long-term career objectives. In this initial conversation, he shared with me the positive feedback he had received on my solid performance and contributions to date. He said that he was impressed to hear that in less than a year I had climbed the learning curve quickly, had made several contributions, and had other projects in progress to deliver even more positive results. After discussing this briefly, he then asked me if I was aware of the company's employee mentoring program. I told him no. He shared the information that it was a program where the company assigns a new, strong individual (mentee) to a proven, more experienced leader (mentor) in the organization, allowing the mentor to share his or her wisdom and experience with the mentee. He stated that though these relationships can evolve naturally and many times do, and though he had the responsibility to train, help, and guide me as my manager, this formal program has also proven to be beneficial to those who have participated in it.

"Cameron, if you are interested," he said, "I would be willing to submit you as a candidate for the program and see if we can get a mentor assigned to you. I am motivated to do this because I am interested in you and your career development. Additionally, the company will benefit from your further developing the necessary skills it takes to be successful in business. Your educational background has prepared you up to this point, but additional business coaching can take you to a higher level if you listen, learn, and apply what is shared. Would you be interested?"

I said, "Absolutely, I am very interested, as I know I have a lot to learn about how to be successful in the business world."

As we concluded our meeting, my manager again welcomed me to his team and said he would set up a mentor/mentee relationship for me in the next several weeks assuming he gained approval. I went back to work and was feeling good about the positive feedback I received from my new manager and was very excited about the offer to get engaged in the employee mentoring program and the opportunity to learn from a more experienced business leader in our company.

Chapter 2

An Introduction to My Mentor

Weeks seem to fly by when you are busy working on your assigned projects. In an unscheduled meeting about two weeks from our first discussion on the employee mentoring program, my new manager and I went to a small conference room as he wanted to share an update on the topic. He started enthusiastically, saying, "Cameron, I have some good news and some more good news for you! The good news is that we are moving forward with your mentoring, as you have been approved to participate in the program, and the additional good news is that your assigned mentor is one of the best, highly respected individuals in our company. Your assigned mentor's name is Kenneth, and I have already arranged your first meeting with him tomorrow." Impressed by the speed in which this process was moving, I told my manager that I appreciated his efforts and that this was exciting news. I was happy to get started and felt fortunate that I had been approved and assigned to one of the best mentors in the company to help me on the enhancement of my business skills.

As I entered the scheduled conference room to meet with Kenneth the following day, he was already sitting there with a smile as he welcomed me with a warm hello. He asked me to sit down and said we would go right to work. Kenneth started, "Cameron, congratulations on being approved for the employee mentoring program. I challenge you to listen, take notes, research, and practice what I will share with you over the next fourteen sessions. I say fourteen because although I love mentoring and coaching the newer employees in the company, I still have a full-time job. I will meet my mentoring commitments but will do so in a very methodical, scheduled way, ensuring that I continue to meet my business deliverables as well. I think coaching is an investment in the company's future through sharing information and experiences with the company's number one asset—the employee. As a result, Cameron, this first session will be focused on our introduction and our meeting schedule. Our next meeting will cover the process I use to coach mentees and an introduction to the specific skills I focus on during the remaining thirteen one-on-one sessions. I use the words mentoring and coaching interchangeably but actually prefer the word coaching, as I am a sports lover and think coaches add so much value by providing guidance to their teams. That is the role I fill in this relationship. You will have to absorb the information, apply it to your environment and business experiences, and actually do the work.

"Regarding our schedule Cameron, I would like for you to plan a one-hour meeting with me weekly for the next fourteen weeks. Normally Friday afternoon is a good time for us to meet. Some sessions will probably take all sixty minutes while others may take a little less, but each will be packed with information and experiences that help in meeting business objectives and enhancing your career. Cameron, again, I want to congratulate you on being part of this valuable program. I look forward to mentoring and coaching you. I guarantee that the information I share with you will help enhance your career if you choose to study and continuously practice each skill."

I replied with a thank you and said that I was truly looking forward to listening, learning, taking notes and applying what he had to share.

Chapter 3

The Mentoring Process and the Thirteen Skills

As we entered a room the next Friday for our first formal mentoring session, I asked Cameron if he had ever heard of Benjamin Franklin's personal development process. He replied that he had not. "Well, as you study the subject of success, which certainly will be one of the practices you will need to develop if you want to become successful, you will study how other successful people accomplish what they accomplished. In my research on this topic, I discovered many years ago that Mr. Franklin established a personal development process that is extremely easy and flexible. I decided to use that process myself in many areas of my life and now use Franklin's process to share the business skills I challenge all my mentees to learn and practice."

"Mr. Franklin's process uses the calendar quarter and identifies thirteen skills, traits, or habits one wants to develop and researches, studies, and practices one of them for a week at a time and repeats that process four times each year. Not only is it important that you learn the skills that I am going to recommend you develop but also that you understand, adopt, and practice this process of focusing on one skill per week for thirteen weeks and repeat that effort four times each year. That way you not only learn but also internalize each skill you are trying to develop and ultimately make it part of your natural response to the business environment you find yourself in at the time. Cameron, my coaching style is to empower or enable you to achieve success by sharing this practical process and thirteen very important business success skills. It is *your* responsibility to practice the process, study and implement the skills, embrace each as your personal philosophy, and work them into your daily habits.

"I will share the thirteen skills I will challenge you to develop and internalize in a minute, but let me say a couple of things prior to actually getting into the specific skills. First of all, all these skills are what I call *transferable skills*. They will work in your current job, they will work in your next job, and they can be transferred to most if not all jobs and work environments you will ever find yourself in. Second, these skills will be mostly business focused, thus supporting the company's employee mentoring program. However, weaved into my philosophy is an important *balance* between your work life and your home life. I have seen both 'workaholics' and others who have found a better balance between their work demands and their home life. Without exception, those who found a balance of the two were happier overall and more productive in the long run.

"Now that I have shared Mr. Franklin's simple personal-development process, let me share some information that will help you implement the process more easily throughout your life. Our focus is success—your success! I have a definition I want to share with you that I learned from Jim Rohn. Mr. Rohn defines success as the steady progress toward your own personal goals. He pushes his students to set up their own definition and not some stereotypical definition society may be advertising at the time. One of your assignments is to start working on your very important, very personal success definition.

"Once you establish how you define success in all key areas of your life, here are three ingredients that you need to know to help you actually achieve those definitions. First of all, you need to recognize your greatest power. The greatest power that we all have is the *power of choice*. Too many people do not think about nor leverage this fact. The secret is to acknowledge this significant power and utilize it to your advantage. I couple this next ingredient with the power of choice, and that is that *what you think about* most of the time will come into your life. If you think positive thoughts, that is what you will experience; if your thoughts are negative, then that will be the environment you will create. As I share these thirteen skills and as you practice the weekly process, I want you to choose to think about the specific skill, what it means, and how it applies in business and specifically in your current job. I want to challenge you to think about how to expand each skill and creatively use each skill in your business and personal life. As you choose to think about these skills more and more, they will naturally expand into your life and become part of how you think, act and naturally respond. When you achieve that level of use of these skills, then you will enjoy true success. The last of the three ingredients is the concept of *working*. Zig Ziglar put it so well that I will not try to top it with a phrase of my own. Mr. Ziglar said that the greatest ideas, tools, skills, etc., will not work unless you do! A key ingredient of everyone who was ever successful at what they pursued, Cameron, was their willingness to *work*. Always be ready to *work* for what you want. Another good phrase from Mr. Ziglar on this point is 'Success is 10 percent inspiration and 90 percent perspiration.'

"Cameron, let me close today's discussion by providing you the list of thirteen skills I will cover with you. I will share one skill each week for the next thirteen sessions. My thirteen skills that will enhance your career are:

Dedicated to Serving Your Customers

Honesty and Integrity in the Business World

Career-Focused Goal Setting

Optimism

Optimizing Quality *and* Quantity

Going the Extra Mile

A Career with Balance

Balance through Time Management

Persistence

Working with Others

Lifelong Learning

The Serenity Prayer

Results

"I will reinforce Mr. Franklin's process by practicing it in our weekly mentoring sessions. I ask you to develop that single skill, have a weekly focus, and make it a part of your life. I would note that part of the beauty of Mr. Franklin's process is that you can use it on these thirteen skills as well as exercise it with other skills in completely different areas you decide to develop in the future. You are young and have a lot of opportunity in front of you. This process can be a handy tool that you can add to your tool box. Lastly, I have found that using what I call reminder phases is a good way to reinforce a specific skill. So in addition to providing information about each skill, I will close each session by sharing four reminder phrases you can note and memorize over time to help recall each skill's message."

Chapter 4

Dedicated to Serving Your Customers

Courteous treatment will make a customer a walking advertisement.

—*James Cash Penney*

Cameron and I met at the conference room for our scheduled Friday mentoring session and before we even sat down, I asked, "Cameron are you in sales?" Though I knew Cameron was not in a sales department, I wanted to get him thinking about that question. Cameron replied that he was not in sales.

"Today I am going to introduce to you the first of the thirteen key business skills needed to be truly successful in your career. I asked if you are in sales, and your reply was no. From now on I want you to change your response to that question and always respond with 'Yes, I am in sales,' as we are all in sales. The first skill you need to develop is that of being *dedicated to serving your customers.* All successful companies are dedicated to taking care of their customers. As long as companies take care of their customers, efficiently of course, they will be in business and will see their business grow. Those companies who do not take care of their customers slowly or sometimes quickly experience failure.

"The sales department is the function that links most organizations' customers to the company, but a successful company believes that all their employees are in sales—selling their company's products, services, and reputation. This is why I want you to always think you are in sales. It may be indirectly, but if you are not positively impacting the company's customers in some way, I would say your job is not needed!

"The philosophy is that no matter what role you have in your company, they all roll up to meeting your customers' needs one way or another. There are direct and indirect customer interfaces, but all jobs are there to serve your customers. One way I have seen this used, Cameron, is by seeing all external customers as the 'Big C' and defining all internal customers as the 'Little c.' Have you ever heard of Malcolm Baldridge?" Cameron said he had not. "Well, Mr. Baldridge was the secretary of commerce from 1981 to 1987 and led in the creation of a national quality award that was signed into law in 1988 allowing U.S. companies to compete for the top business award in the United States. I will not share the details about the Malcolm Baldridge National Quality Award, but there is something I want you to know about it. Mr. Baldridge used the award and its scoring process as a way to send a strong message to all U.S. companies that one of the key deliverables of any successful company is to focus on taking care of its customers.

"In your career you will have many different jobs, and each will be in some way in support of the company's customers. Zig Ziglar says it this way: 'You can have anything in your life that you want as long as you are willing to help enough other people get what they want.' That's a great summary on this topic and a power-packed statement that I completely agree with. To break it down, first of all it says it's okay to be successful and it's okay to get rich, but in business and in life it has to be at *the service of others*. Success cannot be driven by greed or at the expense of others. That is not right nor how life works and will not be sustainable.

"Cameron, there are many books, articles, etc., on the topic of putting the customer first, and I recommend that you continue to think about this fundamental business skill and research it more until it becomes part of your everyday philosophy, behavior, and decisions. Let me close this first skill with this message. Certainly most would agree that taking care of your customers is the right thing to do. However, what is your and your company's position if faced with an issue that will cost significant time, resources, and money to resolve? What is the right, long-term answer?"

Cameron replied, "Take care of the customer!"

"Yes, that is the right answer but if you were faced with a million-dollar issue that will take twelve months or more to resolve, what do most companies do? Cameron, there are articles and case studies on this specific topic. These situations happen, and these situations really test the company's position on customer service. You will find in your research that some companies choose to stay focused and live up to their obligations and completely take care of their customers, and to my surprise some companies will not.

"In almost all cases the companies who 'take the hit' for their customers, though financially painful in the short term, build even stronger customer loyalty and respect. They know long term it is the right thing for their customers and their business. Start internalizing this success philosophy, and we will move to the second skill next week. Have a great weekend.

"Cameron, note the first set of four reminder phases for the skill of being dedicated to serving your customers listed below. With each of the remaining twelve skills I will also have a set of reminder phrases for you to use in each of the next four quarters over the coming years. I hope you start with these and through your own research add additional phrases that will help you internalize each skill I will share with you."

Reminder Phases:

Q1: Your success is determined by the problems you solve for others.

Q2: Give your clients something they cannot find anywhere else and they will keep returning.

Q3: Currents of favor begin to flow the moment you solve a problem for someone.

Q4: The most successful individuals are those who serve the greatest number of people.

Chapter 5

Honesty and Integrity in the Business World

The success family is made up of work as its father and integrity as its mother.

—Zig Ziglar

As I met with Cameron to discuss the second skill, I was thinking that weeks seem to pass quickly when you are busy. I started off by bridging from last week's discussion. "Cameron, being dedicated to serving your customers was the first business skill I shared as I think it's the most important. Recall that I closed our discussion about big decisions companies need to make occasionally about spending significant resources to solve a problem for their customers and that the right answer was to do the right thing no matter the cost. Well, Cameron, this second business skill is highly correlated to that philosophy, but it will be at a more personal level.

"The second business skill we all have to develop is that of *being honest and having integrity* in your daily business dealings. In today's business world there is a growing number of individuals, at all levels, who lack complete honesty and integrity in their interactions with their customers, business partners, employees, management, and themselves. This trend is driving a higher level of distrust in business, causing the need for costly efforts like audits, investigations, and other techniques of 'making sure' only the highest integrity has been practiced. These costs are unnecessary when you consistently—as in *all* the time—deal honestly. Over time, after years of consistent, honest dealing with your business colleagues, you will develop the necessary reputation of having a high level of honesty and integrity.

"Cameron, like most good things in life, at first it's tough to establish the right, consistent way of thinking and behaving. But once the habit is formed and the personal philosophy has time to mature, sustaining that behavior becomes easier. Establishing a reputation as a businessperson who always deals honestly and has the highest integrity will reward you in many direct and many indirect ways. There are a number of benefits: 1) internally, your reputation will proceed you when you compete for a different job opportunity; 2) externally, the subject of being honest and trustworthy should be brought up during interviews as it's an asset you can bring to that company; 3) respect from your colleagues will be enhanced; and 4) when dealing with external business partners, you will receive better performance due to the respect you have earned by dealing with them with a high level of integrity. Obviously, when you have not been honest in your different business dealings the opposite is true. Dishonest employees will not win in the long run regarding promotions, raises, key assignments, etc. Dishonest people in business do not have the respect of their peers or partners and suffer the consequences their entire careers.

"Though I can tell you already have this skill, I still must include in on my list of thirteen due to its importance. Even if this skill may be one you already practice, I still think it's so important it will always be high on my list of skills one must have in business and in life. Regarding the list of benefits I shared earlier, let me add one more. Another reason I would list for practicing honesty and maintaining high integrity in all your dealings is that if you do not just one time, then you will lose that powerful, valuable reputation for the rest of your career. This skill is so important, because that once it is lost, total trust is never ever regained.

"Cameron, you know by our earlier discussion that a significant part of this personal-development process is for you to take these fundamental business skills and thoroughly research and gain additional insight and information on each. I predict that on this topic many of the stories and case studies you review will be negative examples. I want to share one that is negative, but I do that to provide an example for you to learn from, for we can learn from both positive and negative examples.

The one example I will share is about a seemingly successful energy company in Houston, Texas, with stock prices at $90 per share in mid-2000. The horrifying and almost unbelievable story at Enron involved several of Enron's top executives, many of whom are serving prison sentences, and an independent consultant paid to keep this exact behavior from occurring. These individuals were so warped in their thinking that their inaccurate financial reporting and incorrect accounting practices ultimately drove the company into bankruptcy by the end of 2001 when their stock price hit less than $1.00 per share. None of these individuals, all highly educated and experienced, started their dishonest thinking and behavior only in this situation. No, I would say that each started just stretching here and there on some of their operational performance measurements, creatively updating their presentations to make this or that parts of their business not look so bad. As they grew in the company and in their responsibilities, this incorrect, dishonest line of thinking simply continued. This huge bankruptcy case is an extreme example, but my point here is that the dishonest line of thinking and behaving does not usually start big—it starts small and grows. I challenge you to be one of the honest examples in business and be part of the fight against negative practices.

"Cameron, in closing let me share a few examples I have seen over the years that seem to be 'part of doing business,' yet I would say are examples of lack of honesty and dealing only with the highest of integrity. A short list of examples include: a) when sharing performance measurements, 'rounding up' or packaging the measurement so that they look better than they really are—this is where the phase 'liars figures and figures lie' comes from; b) a salesperson exaggerating his or her progress with a prospect or stretching the company's product capability to help make the sale; c) project managers claiming project completion is further than it is; and d) claiming closure of key deliverables when actually several key elements of the deliverable remain open. I will finish, Cameron, with an example that virtually everyone gets exposed to in their careers, and that is not meeting their commitments. This practice of missing commitments seems to occur all too often. One could argue that missing a commitment is not being dishonest, and in most cases I would agree. I do believe, however, that developing a reputation of missing commitments can be harmful to your career. Therefore, my recommendation here is simple—meet your commitments, and on the occasion that a deliverable will be missed, communicate to whomever you have that commitment with that you need to establish a new completion date and communicate that prior to the original due date. Then meet that new date. A common phase used in business is 'under commit and over deliver.' Try not to 'sandbag' or under commit so much—it's too conservative. Do not overdo the 'under commit' philosophy or another unattractive reputation (sandbagger) will develop. Rather, learn to overachieve on the deliver side of this simple equation. Cameron, if over the years you develop a reputation of honesty, high integrity, and of being someone who can be counted on to meet his commitments, you will be highly respected by customers, peers, and management and highly rewarded as well.

"We took the entire hour today; think about this skill and I will see you next week."

Reminder Phases:

Q1: Your integrity will always be remembered longer than your product.

Q2: Be a person of excellence and integrity, which is the foundation of success. Be truthful even if it hurts, even when no one is watching.

Q3: Better is the poor that walketh in his integrity than he that is perverse in his lips and is a fool (Proverbs 19:1).

Q4: If what you say to someone cannot be said to everyone, then say it to no one (J. E. Murdock).

Chapter 6

Career-Focused Goal Setting

Success: The steady progress toward your own personal goals. —*Jim Rohn*

After Cameron and I took our seats to discuss the third skill, I said, "There will be a couple of themes that you will detect throughout our discussions, and one of those themes is *balance*. In fact, skill number seven will be all about balance. That theme is seen in this session as well. The third skill I want you to focus on is that of consistently setting and documenting specific *career goals*. Cameron, before we discuss career goals specifically, let me provide you with a brief overview of the powerful practice of setting goals.

"Goal setting is a very, very powerful tool and practice in the pursuit of success. In fact, goals are a prerequisite for success. I know you well enough to know that you have already set and achieved many goals in your young life. Goal setting is one of those subjects with a lot of books and other material available for you to research and study. To add to your current goal-setting tool box, let me share the following guidelines of setting goals before we specifically talk about career goals: 1) your goals should be balanced across at least these seven areas of your life—spiritual, mental growth, physical health, family, career, financial, and social contribution (Zig Ziglar); 2) your goals should be yours and no one else's; 3) your goals should be written; 4) your goals should be specific, personal, positive, and in the present tense; 5) you should have both short-term (< one year) and long-term (> one year) goals; 6) goals must be conceivable, believable, achievable, and controllable by you; 7) state them with *no* alternative; 8) be sure there are some significant, tough, long-reaching, *big* goals on your list; some of your goals need to stretch you; 9) prioritize your goals and make sure they are consistent and compatible with each other; 10) share them only with others who can help you achieve them; 11) make sure they are measurable with deadlines; and 12) review and update your goals regularly (at least every six months).

"Cameron, I encourage you to actively set goals in all areas of your life, but my focus today will be to help you set and focus specifically on career goals. First of all, if you analyze the available hours you have each week (one week is 168 total hours) and if you only work forty hours, that makes up 24 percent of your total available hours. If you work forty-five hours, that would be about 27 percent; and if you worked fifty hours in a week, that would be 30 percent of your total available hours in a week. The time you spend at work is a significant percent of your total hours in a week. To further emphasize this point, if you eliminate the fifty-six hours of sleep from the equation, then work becomes an even more significant part of our lives, making fifty work hours equate to 45 percent of our week that we are awake. Given the significant amount of time you spend at work, your career goals need to ensure that you are working on what you enjoy working on. The following phrase will capture that message: 'There is nothing worse than climbing the ladder of success only to find out that it is leaning against the wrong wall.' Additionally, if you add the time for preparation and commute, it only further reinforces the point that we spend the majority of our non-sleeping hours working on our careers. Thus your career objectives must be well thought out, documented, and updated as the years pass.

"In my studies of this skill, I heard an executive of a large newspaper asked, 'How did you achieve your position?' The executive simply responded, 'I wanted it and I worked hard to obtain it.' Cameron, to climb the ladder of success you have to decide what you want to do and work hard at attaining it. Here is the process I recommend you follow for setting your career goals. Start by deciding what job you want to retire from or end your career doing. Yes, a tough question to answer at a young age but a very important one. Hold that job and its responsibilities along with its rewards in your mind. That goal may be twenty, twenty-five, or thirty years away, but even if you updated it during your career, always have that last job in mind. Next, establish a ten-year job goal; then a five-year job goal; and finally identify your very next job. Each of these jobs should be specific, and each should build on the other to complement and support your competing for and achieving that last position you see yourself holding. Each of these goals should be documented in your career-development plan. However, the next job you want should be documented with more specifics, including the job title and the unique skills you need to develop for that specific position. As you analyze the skills you need, list the ones you already have and the new ones you need to develop to earn that next position. Ensure that part of your plan is to gain experience and develop skills in those areas where you have had limited exposure. One way to achieve this without changing jobs is to accept special assignments in the areas you need that additional experience. Equally important is to continue to strengthen your existing skills while you add these new skills to your résumé. As new skills are developed, be sure to document them on your résumé, always having it updated and available for that next opportunity. I also recommend that your immediate manager and his or her manager know your desires—but only share with those individuals who can and will help you achieve that next specific job.

"On the sensitive subject of timing of these job moves, I would recommend this: you should commit to any job for at least one year and plan to pursue that next job between years one and two. I used the word sensitive because if you are going to have a lot of different jobs in your career, you will also have a lot of different managers. You will find that each of these managers will have a different perspective as to 'your availability' and when they will let you compete for your next opportunity. This is why I said earlier you should plan on at least a year, as you should 'pay them back' for hiring you to your current position. All new jobs have learning curves (if not, do not take it as it would add no value to your skill base), and you need to deliver some results before you can expect to be allowed to compete for that next opportunity. Cameron, on the subject of timing there are three practices I will suggest to help you: First of all, since you already know what that next job is, share that objective with your new manager within the first couple of months on the current job. Second, develop skills to climb learning curves quickly. Usually that requires more time at work initially, so plan around the fact that for several months after taking a new position, you will have to put in some extra time and effort just to get back to that same level of competence you were at in the previous position. Last, and the most obvious, produce significant results in that current job. Results will earn you the support of your current manager and the right to ask to move on and prepare you to compete against others for that next position.

"As we close, let me say that there are some levers in this process you can control, including the skills you have, specific goals you set, your detailed plans, work effort, and your contributions. There are, however, some things you do not have control over, for example, current economic environment, where the company is at in the industry its growth curve, and your direct competition. I recommend that you only focus your time and energy on those things you *can* control. Acknowledge that those other uncontrollable factors will impact you sometimes—for example they may delay your next move—and be patient and mature enough to accept those facts when they occur. Cameron, that completes are discussions on career goal setting, I hope it was beneficial for you."

Reminder Phases:

Q1: William James, a great American psychologist, said about success: "An inner idea which is followed persistently with courage. An outer achievement related to that idea."

Q2: Ask, and it shall be given you; seek, and ye shall find; knock, and it shall be opened unto you (Matthew 7:7).

Q3: Without dreams and vision we perish.

Q4: You will only have significant success with something that is an obsession.

Chapter 7

Optimism: It Can Be Done

If you think you can, or you think you can't, you're right! —Henry Ford

"Cameron," Kenneth started as we gathered for our weekly Friday mentoring session, "do you have your career goals set?"

I responded, "I have thought about them a lot since last week's discussion and have written a few things down, but no I have not completed them."

Kenneth said, reassuringly, "That's okay. Last week I gave you a lot to think about and a lot of homework. I actually did not expect you would be finished yet and am glad you are not, because I want to influence your decisions with the information I will share with you today on the fourth skill.

"The fourth skill you must develop, practice, and continuously improve is the skill of having *optimism*. As you think about your career goals, aim high, be aggressive, think big, and be optimistic that you can achieve them. Cameron, I am not a trained psychologist, but I have studied this concept for years; today I will simply challenge you to be optimistic and become more and more optimistic over time. I want you to increase your optimism year in and year out, and I will share quotes and examples on the topic to help serve as a foundation for you regarding this important and powerful way of thinking.

"I love that quote (above) by Henry Ford. As you study Mr. Ford and the early years of what is now the Ford Motor Company, you will learn a couple of things: 1) Mr. Ford was not the most highly educated individual of his time; and 2) Mr. Ford was, however, one of the most positive and optimistic people who ever lived. Certainly, Mr. Ford had many skills; but his optimism was one skill that helped start and develop his vision of the first motorized vehicle and all its enhancements. It's not what you are (the skills you have) that holds you back (from achieving *big* goals); it's what you think you're not! The message in this powerful saying is that it's your own philosophy, your own lack of optimism and belief in yourself that holds you back from setting and achieving big goals. Cameron, you are remarkable, and you can do remarkable things. If you believe you can achieve your big goals, with optimism and a willingness to work, you undoubtedly will.

"I have seen individuals and teams do remarkable things. Here are a couple work experiences I had in my career. When I was in a materials manager's role in the manufacturing environment, the team hired a new engineering manager. It was at the beginning of the year; and though the engineering team had good leadership and a strong performance record, this new manager expected his team to achieve a 25 percent improvement in *everything* they measured in that calendar year. The engineering team at first was shocked. There was strong pushback with reasons explained why achieving a significant improvement of 25 percent was 'impossible' on many of the engineering deliverables. The 'cannot do' attitude lasted for a month or two. The new engineering manager did not compromise and remained firm on his expectations and his optimism/belief in his team and that the objective could be accomplished. Finally the team stopped fighting the challenge and started working on it. I have to say, I truly enjoyed with amazement watching that strong engineering team transition from disbelief to belief and then to success. Though not every measurement achieved a 25 percent improvement, most did; and some areas achieved over a 40 percent improvement—unbelievable! By the way, that engineering manager, though only in middle management at the time, went on to be a highly paid executive at several very successful companies in his career.

"The second example happened to me and my team. I was managing this team for a period of three years. Though our scope changed a lot over that time, the one key business deliverable and measurement of saving the company money did not. During year one we saved over 10 percent over the spend we had the year prior. In year two we were asked for another double-digit savings and we achieved 12 percent. Then in year three we were asked to save yet another 10 percent! As these aggressive targets were for savings on the previous year's base spend, both the team and I were in denial and pushed back once we received the third annual objective. As time passed the objective did not change. Though still not sold, I started to lead the team to the aggressive objective. As the team and I embraced it and started focusing on obtaining it and not on all the reasons why it could not be done, some positive results started accumulating. As I fast forward this story, I share it with you because though we achieved yet another double-digit saving percentage that third year, what was really accomplished was a very strong personal experience on the topic of optimism and its power. Ever since that experience, my philosophy and leadership style are significantly influenced by the power of optimism—believing it *can* be done!

"Cameron, optimism is a key skill on my list of thirteen skills I will share with you. It's important, it's fun, it's exciting, it's exhilarating, and it's contagious. As you research this skill and further weave it into your everyday philosophy and work behavior, you will see many positive changes, first in yourself and then in those you influence. I position optimism right after goal setting for a reason. If you can see your objective and write it down, no matter what it is, you can achieve it. You just need to believe in yourself and be optimistic that it will happen. Between now and next week, keep working on honing in on your career goals and know that you can and will achieve them. We'll meet again next Friday."

Reminder Phases:

Q1: Whatever your mind can conceive and you can bring yourself to believe, you can achieve (Napoleon Hill).

Q2: Nothing great was ever achieved without enthusiasm. Focus on the last four letters of the word enthusiasm: IASM—I Am Sold Myself.

Q3: I like thinking big. If you're going to be thinking anyway, you might as well be thinking big (Donald Trump).

Q4: Be patient; success does not come overnight. Rather, it takes time, sometimes a lot of time. But if you keep your thoughts optimistic and focused on our objectives and truly believe you can accomplish what you are seeking, you will.

Chapter 8

Optimizing Quality *and* Quantity

But this I say, He which soweth sparingly shall reap also sparingly; and he which soweth bountifully shall reap also bountifully.　—*2 Corinthians 9:6*

As Kenneth and I met in front of the small conference room, he greeted me and asked if I was making progress on my career goals. I said I was and recalled last week's message of optimism and said I was working on my *big* career goals! He smiled as we entered the room.

"Cameron, this week's skill has that *balance* theme in it. Some of the skills I will share with you are learned from others observing and studying the topic. This week's skill, number five on my list, is one that I have learned and developed personally from the very start of my career all the way up to my current position.

"The fifth skill is *optimizing the quality of your work with the quantity of your work.* Throughout your career you will run into both these camps regularly, but less frequently will you run into the philosophy of balancing both. The balancing of these two skills is important and links directly to our first skill of taking care of the customer. Customers, no matter what business you are in, want a company's products or services to be balanced—having a *high value* that meets their needs. Something of value balances both high quality and high quantity. I will not spend much time on how a company also needs to balance and optimize these skills, but I will share information on the importance of you doing it as an individual.

"Before we talk about the balancing and optimization of these two skills, let's talk about each of them separately. We will start with *quality*, which I believe is the right place to start. Your personal output, what you deliver in your job assignment, must always be of high quality. No internal or external customer will want a product or service or any deliverable that does not have high quality. Additionally, as you mature and gain more and more experience, you certainly want the reputation for producing only high-quality work. Let me quickly comment on the fact that sometimes you will mess up—we all do. The key here is to admit it and never cover it up; always fix it, and most important, learn from the mistake and try not to repeat it. Try to put processes in place to help prevent repeating the issue again. Sometimes quality is easily measured; other times it is not. In all cases, set high expectations and drive yourself to achieve those expectations. Especially in those tough-to-measure environments, if you are honest with yourself, you will know what a quality job or output looks like. Set that expectation up in your head and pursue and accept only that high-quality performance. Do this yourself and do not be a follower on setting quality performance expectations—be your own leader. You will become more valuable to all organizations if your quality expectations and performance are high.

"Let's discuss *quantity* by itself for a moment. Quantity can be defined in a lot of different ways in business. In a manufacturing environment it's measured easily in output per minute or hour or day. In a project-management environment it's establishing and accomplishing defined tasks that will accumulate into the completion of a project that adds value to the company's customers either directly or indirectly. Since quantity is measured differently based on the environment, I will link it to the general concept of volume and that more is better and usually higher volume drives lower costs. As you start new jobs, your output or volume will be low, but as you climb the learning curve, your output or volume will increase. Obviously, this skill challenges you to increase your quantity over time and out-produce others doing the same or similar functions. With a focus only on volume or quantity, you can always do more if you sacrifice on the quality side of this equation; and that takes us to the true challenge in this fifth skill—optimizing both.

"As we start talking about how to optimize, let's take the two skills at their extreme to show how one without the other will not work. If you only focus on quality, then your output may be 'perfect' and of the highest quality but the product may be so slowly developed the results will be too late to the market and too expensive. If you only focus on speed, volume and cost then the product or service will be available quickly and be inexpensive but will cause customer dissatisfaction because of poor product quality. Balancing both skills is the only acceptable solution in business.

"As you grasp this philosophy and in time gain personal experience, let me share how you can put it to work and pursue its optimization. The best way to explain this is to assume you are in a new job or were just given a new assignment. My experience says that most customers, managers, and organizations will accept less volume at first but expect high quality from the beginning. Therefore always start slowly and ensure that your output is of high quality. Then over time through experience and better processes, while maintaining the same quality, start increasing the output or volume of your deliverables. Over time you will increase the output while maintaining the expected quality level. As you analyze your work, practice the skill of optimizing these two deliverables and you will increase the value to the job, company, and ultimately the customer. The skill and reputation you want is for others to know that you can, in time, take any job and perform it at both a high level of quality while also producing large quantities of output efficiently. This is a differentiator you want to be known for!

"Let me close this session with two final thoughts. As you continue to drive improved optimization, at some point you will be confronted with the decision to sacrifice quality to gain more quantity (at reduced cost). When you are at that point, you are already performing at a high level. However, if you want to go just a bit higher, I will suggest that it is okay to compromise some quality for more quantity, *but* that compromise in quality has to be at a level that is acceptable to the customer. So at this point in your optimization efforts, always consider what the customer will accept. In fact, they may be more interested in a little less 'quality' for the added benefits of more quantity at a reduced price. This is not an easy analysis and should be approached cautiously, but it is an acceptable solution in some environments. The last point I will share today is that in a lot of jobs, this will be very subjective and tough to measure. I will argue, however, that you still need to assess, even if it is only your gut feeling, whether you are balancing and optimizing the two deliverables.

"Keep the pressure on yourself to always look for more ways to improve quality and quantity and develop ways to optimize both. Make it a personal quest that is fun and you will soon learn that as you improve this skill you will be rewarded for its development. Thanks for your time today, and I am looking forward to sharing the sixth skill with you next week."

Reminder phrases:

Q1: Diligence is speedy attention to an assigned task. It is insistence upon completion.

Q2: If a task is once begun, never leave it till it's done. Be the labor great or small, do it well or not at all!

Q3: The best way to get the next job or a better job is to be the best at the one you have.

Q4: You are never overqualified for a job. Do all jobs well to the best of your ability.

Chapter 9

Going the Extra Mile

Rendering more and better service than you are paid to render, doing it all the time, and doing it with a pleasing, positive attitude. —Napoleon Hill

I began our mentoring discussion the following Friday, with the next important skill, *going the extra mile*. This skill of going the extra mile is not a new concept to you. I am sure you have heard of it and probably practice it.

"You may have heard the saying 'It is never crowded on the extra mile.' The reason it is not crowded is because most people do not perform out there most of the time. This sixth skill is simple in principle but tough in practice. You do not have to go the extra mile to be reasonably successful. That is the space most people perform in. They want to 'get the job done' and 'do a good job' and get paid for what they do. You will find that the majority of the people you work with will be performing with this philosophy. Now, do you think you, or anyone for that matter, will achieve the highest level of success with *just* getting the job done? In any job or task there is always a little bit more that you can do. This skill expects its students to practice three things: 1) develop the philosophy that you need to go the extra mile in almost everything you do; 2) look for that little extra that needs to be done to attain that higher level of achievement; and 3) gladly perform that little extra almost every time. If you practice this skill, it almost single-handedly will propel you forward in your career. Notice I said do this *almost* every time. Let me explain. Practically speaking, throughout your long career there will be times when you will not be able to go that extra mile. There will be situations that just will not allow you to do so. In fact, we will discuss that in detail in our next session. However, I recommend that you habitually observe and think of the opportunities to take whatever you are doing to that higher level every time. Most of the time you can then implement and take action on what you observe, and that is when you will be investing in your future—a very bright future. I would also note that you can practice this skill of going the extra mile no matter the job, your education, or your experience.

"Cameron, I said look for the 'little' extra. That is what is amazing about this skill. It is not like you have to boil the ocean in every situation to earn the 'extra mile credit.' Most of the time, going the extra mile is doing or saying little things that will differentiate you from the crowd. The key to this trait is to develop it early in your career and practice it *regularly* throughout your career. The dividends you will receive from your investment in going the extra mile will occur over time and not immediately. The benefits will come from the cumulative effort you put in by practicing this skill. This is why most people do not practice the skill of going the extra mile. It takes time, it takes personal initiative and persistence, it takes extra effort, and it takes patience, and these are the traits most people do not consistently practice. However, these are exactly the skills that, if practiced, will demonstrate to your customers, management, and the business that you are more valuable than the majority of your colleagues and you deserve the extra business, responsibilities, promotion, and other rewards.

"To close out on this key skill, let me make one final point by asking a question. The question is a short, simple one: Who do you work for? I am not really looking for an answer, I just want you to think about the question and allow me to make this point. Cameron, you work for *yourself!* You and I are both paid by our current employer, but I want you from now on to think that you work for yourself. I work for myself and am currently contracting my skills and abilities to our current employer, who pays me for what I deliver to the company and our customers! I want you to internalize this point for many reasons. First, by thinking of your employment this way, you will more naturally practice this sixth skill more consistently. If you are working for yourself, you will go the extra mile because you will firmly believe that you will personally benefit by doing so; and you will! Now, do not think this is only self-serving and that I think you should not be loyal to your employer—that is not the case at all. I have worked here for over ten years now and am very loyal to our company. But by having this philosophy, I personally perform better; and I bring that same performance to the company, this one, to my last one, maybe to a new one in the future. We both win! It is okay to be self-serving if all parties win. That is the way it should be in business—win-win! Second, the reason you have to develop the philosophy that you work for yourself is to provide yourself the flexibility to contract your skills and abilities to other 'buyers' or other companies and maybe even your own company someday. Again, I am saying to be loyal to the company you work for while you are working for them; but there certainly may be more than one company to work for in your thirty-plus-year career. I have worked for four in my career and have been loyal to each. Another point I would add to this second reason to develop the philosophy that you work for yourself is that when your current employer finds it necessary to take resource actions, cutting pay and even laying employees off, you will be psychologically better positioned to handle that tough environment. You will stay productive and not be paralyzed like so many individuals I have seen in my career. This ability will further keep you from being exposed to being laid off, as you become more indispensable. If that event ever did happen, you would certainly be better prepared to deal with the situation. You will know you are self-employed, have significant skills that many companies need, and will be back in the job market much quicker than if you had not developed this philosophy.

"In closing this simple but important sixth skill of going the extra mile, let me say that though it is easy to do, it's also easy not to do, and I challenge you to develop the philosophy, be creative on those little extra things you can do, and actually perform those extra tasks on a consistent basis. If you practice this skill, Cameron, you will experience what Zig Ziglar always says: 'If you do more than you are paid to do, you will eventually be paid more for what you do!'"

Reminder Phrases:

Q1: Develop the habit of personal initiative—doing things that others do not tell you. Without it you will not rise above average.

Q2: There are not traffic jams along the extra mile (Roger Staubach).

Q3: The best goal and personal philosophies will not work unless you do (Zig Ziglar).

Q4: When you want something you've never had, you've got to do something you've never done!

Chapter 10

A Career with Balance

An intelligent person aims at wise action, but fools start off in many directions. —Proverbs 17:24

As Cameron and I sat down for our discussion of skill number seven, I said that unlike the last several skills, which were specifically focused on your career and your work habits, this skill challenges you to balance your career with your non-work activities. "Cameron, life has to have balance! What I do not want you to think from our discussions and the skills I have and will share with you is that I am only messaging to you to focus on your work, professional skill development, and career enhancement. Sure, most of the skills I will share with you and ask you to study and practice will be career and work oriented; but this seventh skill, *a career with balance*, and a couple of other skills will require you to develop the ability to do more than just work. Individuals who just focus on their work life have it easy; it is actually harder to navigate a successful work life while also balancing it with an equally successful home life.

"Some women, but mostly men, get too wrapped up in their career. Sure, during our normal week we will probably spend around 45 percent of our non-sleep hours at work. If you include time to commute and other time we spend preparing, easily 50 percent of our week we will spend on our work. We will discuss this more in detail in our next meeting. The point I want to make today is that our work is a huge part of our life, time, energy, self-worth, and lifestyle. But it is *not* the *only* part of our life! Regardless of the results of a high salary and financial benefits, what kind of lifestyle is it if we only focus on work? Going back to our skill discussion on optimizing quality and quantity, in that scenario, if you are not balanced, you would have a high quantity (money) but a low quality of life (time and love ones to share it with).

"Cameron, you must have a balance in your life. However, over your long career, the biggest push you will experience, I predict, will be to work more and more. Several elements in our work environment will naturally drive and pressure you to work more. Some of those elements include the business itself, which will ask more of all its employees so they can do more for their customers, stockholders, competition, etc. There will always be more tasks to do than you will have time for, and even practicing the skill I shared with you of going the extra mile drives more time demands. These and other things will naturally push you to potentially put more hours in your work day and week than you should to ensure balance in your life. Thus, to counteract this normal pressure to work more, we have to balance it with another philosophy and skill. That skill is to focus on and constantly develop and improve a balanced lifestyle. This skill is very similar to skill number five—quality and quantity. Recall that that skill challenges you to develop the ability to optimize those two requirements in your work environment. This skill, a career with balance, will challenge you to balance the high demand, constant pull of working more and more with the need and obligation you have to allocate appropriate 'home time' doing the things you need to do based on the current relationships and activities you have away from work. Of course, these demands away from work will change over time, thus driving your need to adapt and change along with them.

"Like all the skills I will share with you, Cameron, this balancing act will not be easy. The best things in life are never easy! However, I promise you that if you practice this skill daily, your overall happiness and lifestyle will be far superior to only focusing on your career, I know from experience. Let me share just some of the 'tricks' or techniques that I have used myself in attempting to gain the right balance between career and home life. This will be a short list that worked for me and my specific work and family life. You will have to develop your own practices and ones that help you achieve the skill of balance in your life.

"First, as I have already shared, I personally did not always achieve balance in my life. The good news is I was only out of balance for about ten years. I am sharing this skill with you and all my mentees so you all can develop the skill of balance earlier in your career and life. When I discovered I was out of balance, the first thing I did was to review my priorities. My specific situation at the time was that I had become a father. This event certainly changed my family dynamics and required an honest update of my priorities. I determined that my family was a higher priority than my work; however, being the breadwinner, earning money remained one of my many responsibilities. I analyzed my personal situation and decided that I could meet most expectations at work and at home by working ten hours a day, five days a week. That number ten is important, and I will expand in detail about that number in the next session, but the point here is that I explicitly decided the exact number of hours I would allocate per day to my work and career. This number will vary by individual, and I am not saying that should be your number, but I do recommend that you establish a specific number to aid in your development of this skill of balance. Some other techniques I used to pull myself from work were to commit to obligations outside of work. As my family grew and became active in sports, I volunteered to be the coach of many of those teams my kids played on. If practice was set to begin at 6:00 p.m. and fifteen little boys and girls are waiting for you, you will leave work in time to make that commitment regardless of whether the meeting is running a little late or if you had not read all of the day's e-mails. I know you are single now and do not have this family demand, but I have seen these same practices used by signing up for a class outside of work or a specific workout time that will motivate you to wrap things up at work and get going, improving balance!

"The examples I listed above are specific. They are examples of setting specific goals and establishing commitments outside of work to aid you in your pursuit of establishing an overall balanced lifestyle. The best general technique I used and want to close with has actually already been mentioned in one of our earlier discussions. Skill number three was about career goal setting where we talked about establishing specific short-term and long-term career goals. However, I also planted the seed with you that career goals are only one of seven areas where you should have specific written goals. Recall that I mentioned that goal setting was a very powerful tool in your pursuit and attainment of success. In that discussion we focused on career goals, but I did note that the practice of goal setting needs to be in seven areas of your life, including spiritual, mental growth, physical health, family, career, financial and social contributions. The practice of setting and actively pursuing goals across all seven areas will help you naturally develop more balance in your life vs. spending all your time on any one thing. This was the number-one tool I used to help me ensure balance and more happiness in my life.

"Cameron, the next skill (time management) will be discussed the next time we meet and is purposely positioned behind this skill of establishing balance in your life. Have a great weekend and begin to think about your priorities and all the things you want to do in life and how you will begin to drive balance across all of them."

Reminder Phrases:

Q1: The door to a balanced success opens widest on the hinges of hope and encouragement (Zig Ziglar).

Q2: Six days shall work be done, but on the seventh day there shall be to you an holy day, a Sabbath of rest to the Lord. (Exodus 35:2).

Q3: Before you embark on your journey toward your objectives, be sure to take time and really evaluate your values, priorities, and goals, and be sure they all are aligned.

Q4: Focus concentration; wherever you are, be there (Jim Rohn)!

Chapter 11

Balance through Time Management

Focus on what is important but not urgent, plan these tasks and complete, as you will always work on urgent tasks that are important.

—Stephen R. Covey

After sitting down for our weekly scheduled mentoring session, I started immediately with skill number eight: *time management.* "Cameron, if I recall where we ended our session last week, we were discussing tools you can use to ensure that you maintain a balanced lifestyle and how goal setting across the seven recommended areas was one of the most useful methods to achieve balance. Coupled with that seventh skill of balance, this skill, time management, will be significant in helping you obtain all of those goals while maintaining the desire for balance.

"Cameron, like many of the skills I will share with you, time management is one about which there is large amount of research and information. I will provide you only a small amount of the seemingly endless information on this important topic. Because of my active personality, desire to be balanced, and thirst to experience many things in my life, I have studied time management thoroughly, always looking for ways to squeeze more activities into my day. Let me share a few key lessons I have learned and practiced on this topic.

"First of all I recommend that you develop an enormous appreciation for time. Time is a gift, and none of us know how much we will have. Some individuals live into their eighties and nineties, while others die at a very young age. Just the fact of not knowing should motivate all of us to establish a personal philosophy on the subject and have a deep appreciation for time. I fortunately learned to respect and appreciate time at an early age, and I recommend that you do the same. Second, you must learn that you will *always* have more things to do than you will have time to do them! For this reason, let me share a list of time-management techniques that you can develop to maximize your productivity in the time you do have. These techniques will be for use in your business environment, but most can also apply to your non-business time-management efforts as well.

1) Plan your five business days by analyzing your twenty-four-hour clock. Start with when you go to bed. How many hours of sleep

to you really need? (Do not scrimp on this; sleep is important.) Then, how much time do you need to get ready in the morning? How long is your commute? (Maximizing this use of this time will be discussed on skill eleven—lifelong learning.) What is the actual amount of time you spend at work—recall that I used ten hours? Those work hours will need to have every minute explicitly planned and documented on your calendar—see number four below. Next, what is your return commute time? How much time do you need for your family to prepare, eat, and clean up from dinner (dinner time is excellent family time)? What is your daily workout time allocation? How much time do you need to get ready for the next day and for bed? The time you have left after all these time slots having been subtracted from the total of twenty-four will be the time you have to spend on the other goals you have established for yourself. I recommend doing this analysis in thirty- to sixty-minute buckets. The following is the same example in numbers: 24 − 8 (sleep) = 16 − 1 (get ready) = 15 − .5 (commute to) = 14.5 − 10 (work) = 4.5 − .5 (commute from) = 4 − 1 (dinner/family) = 3 − .5 (workout) = 2.5 − .5 (prepare for bed) = the remaining time available, or two hours. In this example, you only have two hours left to do all the other goals and activities you have set for yourself. That is not a lot of time, so it must be planned and managed wisely!

2) Look for ways to move closer to accomplishing or at least moving forward on multiple goals during the same time period. My personal example is that I choose to work through lunch most of the time. The goals I move forward on when I work that hour include: a) increasing my family time by one hour by making that 'lunch hour' part of my ten-hour work day; b) allowing me to contribute a total of ten hours to my business activities; c) bringing my lunch so I save money by not buying expensive meals daily, thus complementing my aggressive financial budget; and d) better controlling my calories consumed by packing a healthy lunch, including fruits, which complements my health goals. Therefore these conscious decisions help me to move closer in four important areas of my life (family, work, finances, and health).

3) You must learn to prioritize. You have your goals documented, both professional and personal. Ensure that you are allocating time in both those areas doing the things that need to be done in order to move you ever closer to each one of those objectives. Vilfredo Pareto's 80/20 rule should be used here: what 20 percent of your activities and efforts will reap 80 percent of the results you are pursuing? Learn to search for and focus your energy on that 20 percent of the actions needed to achieve the maximum results. A final recommendation on prioritization is

if you have two actions on your list to complete, always do the toughest one first! The easier one will get done; it is the tougher ones we tend to procrastinate on.

4) Since work time (ten hours in our example) is the biggest portion of our twenty-four-hour day, those ten hours must be planned down to the half-hour detail every work day. The saying I learned from Jim Rohn on this is 'Don't start your day, until it's finished.' I accomplished this by committing that before I leave at the end of each work day, say a Tuesday, I review the schedule for Wednesday and schedule all my top priorities and actions in the time slots available on my Wednesday calendar, noting that there are already some standing, recurring meetings on my Wednesday calendar. Plan tomorrow's key activities in all remaining open time slots. I mean every time slot! If you work from 7 a.m. to 5 p.m., all times during those ten hours should be filled in with the current top priorities prior to leaving for the evening on Tuesday. I then print out my calendar, as it serves as my roadmap of activities for the next day.

5) I recommend being proactive and doing the things you need to do when you need to do them. A lot of people are reactive, and my observations are that they develop a habit of being reactive, always in a bit of a panic and putting themselves under unnecessary pressure. Mr. Covey suggests to plan time and focus

on 'the important but not urgent' actions first. Proactively, I have driven the results the business wanted, but I did it on my planned calendar and with significantly less personal stress. As new, important actions arise, proactively place them on the next open time slot on your calendar, ensuring timely attention and closure.

6) Lastly, on the point that we will always have more tasks to do than time to do them, let me close with this concept I learned from studying Brian Tracy. Mr. Tracy's point is since we cannot get everything done then 'practice proactive procrastination.' Most of the time when the word 'procrastination' is mentioned, it is negative. However, this practice says to consciously procrastinate on less important tasks and actions and focus first and only on those actions that will reap you the greatest results!

"The third and last key message I will share is to reinforce the obvious. Our time should be allocated toward the actions we need to take to deliver results we need to meet our goals. We will talk more about results in a later session, but I just want to share this here. We are pursuing certain specific results; those are the topics (at work and at home) we have to allocate 'buckets' of time to. What I mean by buckets of time is allocating one, two or even three hours at a time to that specific, important topic. For me, after a ten-hour work day, I only had a few hours left prior to bed. As a husband and a father I made sure I spent the majority of the rest of the day on my family goals. By allocating time toward those key objectives, I have been able to enjoy the positive dividends of a balanced lifestyle.

"Cameron, there is much more information I could share, much more information out there on this extremely important skill of time management, I recommend that you start practicing what I have shared with you and begin your own personal research and study on this topic. Next week we will discuss another important skill. Take care."

Reminder Phrases:

Q1: Successful people get ahead during the time that most others waste!

Q2: Time is more valuable than money because time is irreplaceable. You can always make more money; you cannot make more time.

Q3: What counts is not the number of hours you put in but how much you put into the hours.

Q4: Our days are identical suitcases, all the same size. It just seems that some people learn how to put more in theirs than others.

Chapter 12

Persistence

Resolve in advance to persist until you succeed, no matter what the difficulty.
                                                            —*Brian Tracy*

I greeted Cameron as we started this weeks meeting and reinforced our time-management lessons of last week by saying, "I hope you have spent your 168 hours this past week only on those most important areas in your life!

"Cameron, I stated in our last session that I know of and have many books, articles, calendars, and other tools/processes on the subject of time management. In contrast, there is less explicit information on this week's skill, *persistence*, but it is still an important success skill on my list. Today I will share some simple philosophies and a few examples on the skill of practicing persistence and, as always, challenge you to develop, refine, and grow the skill in your thinking and daily practices.

"Zig Ziglar stated: 'The world is tough, but it will be significantly less tough on you if you are tough on yourself.' As you pursue your specific career and personal goals, you *will* experience conflicts, setbacks, and many hurdles. Sometimes those hurdles will drive you to the point of quitting. Some goals, over time, may need reevaluation, resetting, and even changing—all of which are okay. However, most goals you will set should be retained and not abandoned. This is where personal fortitude and the skill of being persistent enter in. One skill, studies show, that most successful people have is the skill of being persistent—the never-say-quit mentality. Famous people like Henry Ford had it. President Lincoln, Benjamin Franklin, Thomas Edison, Lance Armstrong, and a lot less well-known parents who successfully raised good kids practiced the skill of persistence. Benjamin Disraeli was quoted as saying 'Nothing can resist a will which will stake even existence upon its fulfillment.' In many speeches, Jim Rohn stated that the two most powerful words in the English language are 'I will.' The human will is incredible. You will find in your research on this topic that though there may not be books like *101 Ways to be Persistent*, there will be many powerful examples of people of all ages in all walks of life achieving very challenging and difficult goals, overcoming tremendous odds, or sacrificing significantly to achieve something. Though the title of the book, movie, or articles may not have the word persistence in it, the theme is certainly all about this important skill. For example, I read where one day a newspaper man asked Thomas Edison how he finally came to invent the incandescent light bulb. Mr. Edison responded by saying that after failing over and over more than ten thousand times, he finally ran out of ways that it did not work. Ten thousand times—now that is persistence! Another example is that in any book you read about President Lincoln and his life story, you will understand quickly how his persistence in his fundamental beliefs eventually helped him to become one of the greatest presidents our county has ever seen. A business example of persistence is found in a story about Henry Ford and how he expected his engineers to develop the V8 engine. They tried and repeatedly told Mr. Ford that it could not be done. However, Mr. Ford was a persistent man, and, as a result, his company eventually produced the first vehicle with a V8 engine. As you know, one of my practices is the use of written goals and reminder phrases. When hurdles present themselves, I reread my list of goals to reinforce what my current priorities and objectives are and read my reminder phrases to help me get back in focus and over the hurdle.

"Cameron, as you research this skill look for examples of a persistent attitude. Look for the behaviors and tactics these successful individuals practiced. Look for the techniques they used to keep them going when they were down with no hope at the time. Learn from your research; learn from the examples of these persistent attitudes, practices, techniques, and your own personal experiences. Mold all of those together into your personality, and this skill will surely be one that will help you through even the toughest of times as you pursue your goals and objectives. Thank you for your time today, and I will see you in a week."

Reminder Phrases:

Q1: Energy and persistence conquer all things (Benjamin Franklin).

Q2: Persistent, consistent, disciplined hard work is what it's going to take to achieve your goals and objectives (Zig Ziglar).

Q3: Nothing is achieved before it is thoroughly attempted!

Q4: Objectives are achieved by small, disciplined steps. We must be persistent and patient.

Chapter 13

Working with Others

So then, my beloved brethren, let every man be swift to hear, slow to speak, slow to wrath.

—James 1:19

As Cameron and I entered the conference room the following week, I began by sharing that the skill we would cover today is one of those tough skills to teach someone in a one-on-one conversation. However this skill, *working with others,* is too important not to at least identify and share some information about and recommend that you add to your skill base as you gain your own personal experience over time.

"Working with others," I started, "is an obvious skill everyone needs to develop, as there is not a 'one-person team' when it comes to business dealings. When doing business, you are always dealing with others in one capacity or another. If you are in a large company, it is obvious that you deal with many people every day to get your job done. There is no way to do business without dealing with others in any size company. Given that fact, this skill is vital to you in taking care of your customer directly or indirectly, the job you do within your company, and your personal success. Working well with others is a key skill to develop if you are going to be successful in business and in life.

"To help you with this skill, let me share a few different areas that you will need to develop this skill to achieve the greatest results. The first skill in the area of dealing with others I recommend that you develop is to embrace diversity. Embracing diversity will make you, your team, your organization, and your company stronger. Diversity comes in many forms from team members of different sexes, backgrounds, religions, cultures, education, experiences, etc. As you grow in our business experiences, if you embrace these diversities you will find that the objectives you are assigned to accomplish will be done better with more breadth and more completeness. I will note that sometimes having a diverse set of skills and opinions on your team leads to healthy debates and sometimes disagreements, so as the leader, you will have to navigate through those situations and drive for conclusions on the timeline you are targeting.

"The second topic I want to discuss as a subset of working with others is a more personal skill, and that is communications. Like other skills we have discussed during these mentoring times we have had together, there are many books, articles, and the like on improving our communications. I would contend that the reason there is so much information on the topic is because it is so very important. I have seen so many times people being casual with their communication practices. In business there are times when you can be casual in your communications, but I would argue that most of the time you cannot be. If there is one area you need to focus on and be attentive to all the time, it would be in your communications. So, first of all, acknowledge the importance of your communications, commit to study the skill, and then practice what you study. Commit to doing this throughout your entire career.

"Let me note that in business, communications come in many different forms. One type is your verbal communications, the use of words and where and what you emphasize. These skills are all part of an effective delivery. So whether you are having a one-on-one conversation or a small team discussion or are addressing a large group, practice those communications and presentation skills as they are invaluable in the business world. One of the best ways to do that, especially after a formal presentation, is to ask yourself what you could have done better and also ask for feedback and focus on improving any areas where you receive recommendations. The second communication skill we must all continue to hone is written communications. Remember those English classes in school where you asked yourself why do I have to take these classes; I am not going to need them? Well, we have all been there, and maybe that lesson on Shakespeare may not come into play every day in business, but that spelling, those commas, and all the other writing skills are key to effective written communications. The last point on both verbal and written communication skills is that I recommend that you learn to be concise with both. Conciseness is efficient, and efficiency in business is very important. The last area of communication I will mention are nonverbal communications, or what some people call 'body language.' I bring it up because I learned three things about this type of communication: 1) it's real and does exist; 2) reading it is a skill that can be developed; and 3) most notable is that these nonverbal communications seems to be at their peak during times and situations where there are more important, tougher decisions. Since it seems to be most active at these important and tense times, it is obviously beneficial to develop the skill of reading these nonverbal messages from others to help you make more accurate decisions.

"The third and last area I want to briefly discuss with you regarding the skill of working with others is leadership skills. Leadership is a fun and challenging area. First, you must be able to lead yourself. That is why you see most new hires to our company, like yourself, get hired in a non-leadership role initially. We have you contribute as an individual first and demonstrate leadership skill prior to providing you with a more formal opportunity. This role would be in a situation when you have an assignment or project where several other business areas will need to be leveraged to be successful. You have the project leadership role to pull the team together, and only through the team's efforts will that task be completed. This is very common, and being good at this type of leadership will be important to your long-term development and career growth. One of the key practices, especially on informal project-leadership assignments, is to always share with the team when you launch the project what the overall goal is, the key deliverables, and the time line the team has to deliver them. These communications from the project leader are vital to 'kick things off' and to get everyone aligned on the key objectives ahead of them.

"The other leadership role is when you earn the right to lead a team as their manager. This is a very important role, as with this role you not only have responsibility for yourself and the assignments you own but also the team members reporting directly to you. Practices that I will share, especially in this formal leadership position, include repeatedly sharing your *vision* with your team members. Let them know what their roles are on the team and in the company and what their contribution is to the customer. As a formal leader, show optimism in accomplishing your challenging tasks and be positive about the team meeting their objectives. As the formal leader, you are responsible for everything your team does, so behave that way and be totally responsible for all they do and sometimes do not do. Finally, be willing to admit a mistake if you make one. We all make mistakes, but so many leaders feel that they will be perceived as being weak if they admit an error—and I have experienced that the opposite is true!

"Well, Cameron, we are running a bit over on our time today because this topic is so broad. It is so very important to hone your skills of working with others. Best of luck to you in this area, and never stop learning how to become better and better at working with others. We'll meet again next week; it was a great discussion today."

Reminder Phrases:

Q1: Coming together is a beginning. Keeping together is progress. Working together is successful (Henry Ford).

Q2: Deal in reality; be strong but not rude, kind but not weak, bold but not a bully, humble but not timid, proud but not arrogant, humor without folly (Jim Rohn).

Q3: A soft answer turn away wrath, but harsh words stir up anger (Proverbs 15:1).

Q4: The atmosphere you permit determines the product you produce.

Chapter 14

Lifelong Learning

The minimum requirement for success in any field is continuous learning.

—*Brian Tracy*

I started, "I have been thinking a lot about what I would share with you regarding this week's skill—*lifelong learning*", as Cameron and I met in the hall waiting for our room.

We entered our room as our colleagues exited, and I said, "Some of these skills I am sharing with you have many books, articles, stories, and examples available. But with skill number eleven, lifelong learning, there seems to be less available, though this skill is critically important for enhancing your career. I know that once you start focusing on this skill it will quickly drive you to continue the practice of lifelong learning for the rest of your days.

"Cameron, on the skill of lifelong learning I will share the following five thoughts with you. First of all, by the skill's name—lifelong learning—the message is clear that learning that starts at birth should end only at death. I have found that many individuals give this skill lip service but do not actually proactively practice it. I want you to be different. Let me say that I am not talking about going back to school or staying in some kind of formal training environment for the rest of your life. What I am saying is to change your philosophy or maybe to establish your philosophy on this topic of learning. I recommend that philosophy to be one that is always open to learning. Know that you will never know it all, that there is always something more to learn, and that you can learn from every situation, experience, and person you interact with. It is not rocket science. It is very simply to establish the philosophy and attitude and actually practice the process of being open to learning a little something every day in every situation.

"Second, I said I do not mean one has to attend formal training all the time, yet having a plan to gain another degree or certification in your profession is a very good goal and certainly a way to add to your lifelong learning practice. A less formal way, yet equally effective, is to practice what Zig Ziglar calls 'automobile university.' I practiced going to automobile university my entire thirty years of working. This is the habit of simply listening to educational CDs in your car while commuting to work. Think about it. If your commute is sixty minutes round trip but you only listen one way each day, the lifelong learning skill is practiced 2.5 hours per week. Cameron, we work around fifty weeks a year. If one were to practice this skill every work week, you could accumulate 125 hours of learning each year! I know there is sports talk and lots of music you would miss, but the skills learned from these professionals will get you promoted, where the latest statistics on your favorite pro team will not. Cameron, I practiced this regularly. I strongly recommend that you pick up this habit as well to enhance your own personal development and career.

"Interestingly, the third way I recommend that you practice this ongoing learning process I learned from listening to a CD. This technique is to identify a skill you want to improve that is meaningful for your current job or the next job and then find the individual in the organization who is the best at that skill. Approach that person and ask if he or she would mind sharing the practices they use to perform so well. I used this technique many times. It is actually complimenting the person when you approach him or her with this request, and I have always had a very positive response from each of my experiences with this practice. By repeating this process throughout your career, you will continue to build a stronger and stronger skill base by learning the important skills from the very best in the business.

"A fourth way I recommend enhancing your skill of lifelong learning is to develop a personal reminder phrase on the topic, and while in your meeting, conference, team, or individual interactions, use a phase like 'What can I learn here?' or 'What can I learn from this?' I recommend something simple and short but just a reminder that will help you stay aware and open to learning something right then. This simple reminder stated silently many times a day will open your mind like a funnel, and you will not believe what all will pour into it. As you practice this fourth technique for lifelong learning, you will be more open in every situation you find yourself in during the day. You will pick up information here and then some more there, and as you align all this input in your head, you will develop a more thorough understanding of that piece of the business.

"Last but not least, you can always learn from yourself! This is a practice that I have seen some people do but not enough nor as frequently as I recommend. The perfect example of this practice is that any sports team that wants to get better will tape their games. Then they review the tapes and look for opportunities to improve. You can do this after any interaction but certainly after some of your more formal reviews or presentations with your boss or after a key meeting with your project teams. Take some time afterward and evaluate yourself or ask a team member for feedback. I have seen sales professionals do this. They say after an important sales presentation, *how did I do?* What a great question: 'How did I do?' Perform this simple, personal, or team practice of ongoing self-assessments. Take what you conclude and learn from these valuable experiences. As simple as this practice is, it can have profound affects in the practice of lifelong learning and professional improvement. It's also easy. This simple practice can be a huge differentiator for you. Let's look at a few numbers. Say you performed this self-assessment two times per day and only four days a week. If you work fifty weeks that year, that equals four hundred proactive learning opportunities you could provide yourself. Cameron, in ten years only a third of a normal career would total four thousand learning opportunities! That is huge, it does not cost any money, and you do not have to drive to a class, yet the personal benefits and ongoing dividends are real! One more thing: in a more challenging area like presenting in front of a large group, you might coordinate beforehand with your boss or a trusted colleague and ask him or her to evaluate your performance and provide both some positive and constructive feedback. However you choose to practice this technique, you will learn that it is simple yet powerful.

"Cameron, I hope you practices some or all of these great techniques to help you continue your lifelong learning. Whichever ones you choose to practice, please practice them religiously and I am confident you will be happy you did. Have a great week, and I am looking forward to our next session."

Reminder Phrases:

Q1: The first step toward success is the willingness to listen.

Q2: A wise man will hear and will increase learning; and a man of understanding shall attain unto wise counsels (Proverbs 1:5).

Q3: The quality of your preparation determines the quality of your performance.

Q4: Someone has heard what you have not; someone has seen what you have not; someone knows what you do not. Your success depends on your willingness to be mentored by them.

Chapter 15

The Serenity Prayer

Learn to be able to distinguish what is in your control from what isn't.

This Friday we met in the cafeteria for this week's session as all of our normal conference rooms were booked. As usual I started right in on the mentoring message for the week. "This week's 'skill' is actually a short prayer—*the Serenity Prayer.* Though I am sure you are aware of the Serenity Prayer, you may not know why I would include it in my list of thirteen skills that I recommend you learn, study, and practice in order to enhance your career.

"Let me explain why the Serenity Prayer—God grant me the serenity to accept things I cannot change, the courage to change the things I can, and the wisdom to know the difference—is on my list. I am assuming that you will work at least thirty years; in doing so, you will work around 7,500 days. You will have some tough days somewhere over that time period. In fact, you will have many days, weeks, and probably months that will require some additional drive, motivation, and acceptance. By regularly reciting the Serenity Prayer, it will help you through those tough times. I prayed it almost daily while driving to work in my early days. Now I only occasionally have to recite it to enjoy its benefits as it's now embedded into my personal philosophy.

"Cameron, no matter how positive you are and even though we have our career goals set and are focused on them, there will be some rocky roads. As we deal with always increasing customer demands, growing business pressures for cost reductions, and competition, suppliers, and all the individuals you interact with, you will find that praying and internalizing the Serenity Prayer is a wise long-term business skill to practice.

"I would not expect you will need this skill for quite some time, but it is always good to have the right tool in the tool box for when you do need it. Let me break this short, simple, yet powerful prayer down a bit. I usually go in reverse order, starting with 'and the wisdom to know the difference.' Wisdom comes with time, experience, and the skill we discussed last week—lifelong learning. One can never have enough, and we should always want more and more. Wisdom is valuable and can never be taken from you. They can take your job, they can shut the doors, and the company can be bought out, but you will always have your wisdom. So we start with being wise. Be wise in your dealing with the many different situations, demands, people, and problems. As you have these experiences, use your growing wisdom to determine how to properly react and respond to the many different scenarios you experience.

"Staying in reverse order, once we have a base of wisdom, you need 'the courage to change the things you can ...' Given your current business situation—no matter what it is—using your accumulated wisdom, assess if it is in your power to change the situation. Obviously, if it is in your power to change it, have the courage to take ownership and develop the plan of action to do just that and then take those needed actions to resolve the situation.

"Lastly, 'God grant me the serenity to accept the things I cannot change ...' I love the word 'serenity.' Just saying it is stress relieving. If in all your wisdom and after thorough analysis you determine that you cannot change whatever difficult situation you are faced with at the time, then pray for serenity to accept the situation and move on. Sometimes praying and saying I am going to accept the situation is difficult. Cameron, I struggle with this 'acceptance' at times, but I have experienced more and more serenity over my career as a result of remembering, saying, and practicing this great prayer. I have shared this advice with all of my mentees and many others individuals and colleagues whom I have observed needed to say and practice this prayer.

"Cameron, as I always do with my mentees on this skill, let me share one more observation I have made regarding the Serenity Prayer. The middle phrase 'and the courage to change the things I can' I have found can be accomplished most of the time. If one would force me to a percentage on this, I would say around 90 percent. Yes, if we are honest with ourselves and are willing to take complete responsibility for our careers and each situation we are in, then I would argue we can 'change' at least 90 percent of the challenges we face, and we must have the courage and willingness to do so. That does leave 10 percent that we do have to practice accepting, and that is okay. Thus, I ask you, Cameron, to gain the wisdom, thoroughly search for creative solutions, and then act on those solutions to resolve the issue, and if that unique situation cannot be controlled by you, accept that fact and move on with serenity.

"Well, Cameron, I have only one more skill to share with you next week, and then we will have a wrap-up session the following week. Our time together has gone by fast. Take care and enjoy your weekend."

Reminder Phrase:

(Repeat all four quarters):

Q1: The Serenity Prayer

Q2: God grant me the *serenity* to accept things I cannot change …

Q3: the *courage* to change the things I can …

Q4: and the *wisdom* to know the difference.

Chapter 16

All That Matters Is Results

The numbers tell the story!   —*Jim Rohn*

As I greeted Cameron with a smile, I said, "Well, Cameron, are you ready to discuss the last skill? Skill number thirteen is the skill of achieving *results*. Cameron, in business, *results is all that matters!* We are paid for getting results, not just being busy. You must develop the habit of completing tasks on time. We have talked about other skills—ensuring that you and the business put the customer first, ensuring that you have your personal career goals established, learning to deal effectively with others, etc. Of course, I would not have shared those skills with you if I did not think they were required to enhance your career. However, at the end of the day if you, your department, and the company do not achieve the business results expected, then you will not be in business long enough to serve your customers. My message to you on developing the skills of delivering results is not meant to be cold, harsh, or impersonal. But the fact is that in business we are employed and paid to help the company make money.

"Though there are many ways to explain the skill and concept of achieving results in business, I will approach it at an individual level. I will focus on how this skill needs to be accomplished by you individually in your current job assignment and responsibilities. However, as you research, study, and practice this skill on an individual level, I challenge you to translate what you learn into how it applies at a department, larger organization, and company level. The skills, techniques, and practices of achieving results as an individual can also be effectively applied with equal success at a broader level.

"Cameron, as you study this skill of achieving results, you will find that there is an endless list of techniques and practices. I will share a process I use to help you get started on this important skill. The way I explain it is for you is to visualize a circle and practice with discipline each of these seven steps on the circle in the following sequence: 1) annually establish and write down the objectives and results you are responsible for achieving and the time frame in which you are to achieve each (business goals); 2) develop a few measurements that will track whether you actually achieve the expected results, making sure each measurement has a specific target (metrics); 3) develop an action or project plan toward the achievement of your desired results (project plan); 4) work to close each action on the plan in the required sequence and time frame (take action); 5) track your progress at the appropriate frequency, sometimes daily, weekly, and monthly, on your performance against each target (feedback); 6) if your feedback has you behind in any way, perform a root cause analysis and develop corrective actions on any objectives not on target to be achieved in the time period established (RC/CA); if you are on or above target, keep doing what you are doing; 7) lastly, whether it's quarterly, semi-annually, or annually, do a complete assessment of your accomplishments, using your metrics to tell you your results against each objective (self-assessment). Be totally honest and objective in this assessment. This process is simple to do but also is simple not to do. Practice this methodology with discipline and you will experience, as I have, that it will serve you well.

"Before we leave this simple yet effective process, let me expand on two points. One, on the root cause, corrective action step, you have to analyze what the reasons are for why you are not at or above your targeted objective at that point in time. By doing this analysis accurately, you will position yourself to get back on track quickly. I would note that the Pareto Principle (or 80/20 rule) needs to be leveraged here. For example, if there are, say, ten reasons why you are currently off your target, you will want to document and implement corrective actions on the top two or three issues creating the biggest hurdles. Focusing on the top 20 percent of the list of issues will allow you to gain 80 percent of the benefits you need to get your results equal to or above target quickly. The second point is that of the concept of continuous improvement. Again, whether this process is exercised quarterly, semi-annually, or annually, it will help you achieve your desired results through its natural process of driving continuous improvements. As targets are achieved and results are delivered, additional goals and/or higher targets need to be established in each of those key business areas. This practice places positive pressure on you and the business. Positive pressure is good! It will not only enhance your career but will also help you gain the needed business results to keep the doors open to your many satisfied customers.

"As we close our discussion today, let me warn you about a situation that occurs in business. I have seen many times where individual's, department's, and company's measurements are either too subjective or are the wrong measurement and are driving the wrong behavior. Your measurements are very, very important. After a measurement review, if you determine that you have the wrong measurements, then change them! Make sure your metrics drive the right behavior from you and your teams. Your deliverables must be measureable. All important business deliverables can be measure objectively with numbers. The disciplined use of measurements takes all subjectivity and emotion out of the situation. Too many times I have seen people use a story to explain why they missed this deliverable or are behind on a metric. A key phrase, from Jim Rohn,

I want you to remember is, 'the numbers tell the story.' So establish those key measurements and track the numbers. If you like the numbers you see as they are at or above aggressive targets, then celebrate and keep it up. If you do not like your numbers, then analyze and develop plans to improve them.

"Cameron, I know on this skill we were very focused on business results, and that is the key message I wanted to share with you in this session. However, like we discussed earlier, you must have balance in your life to be totally happy. I will conclude this discussion with asking you several questions in each of the seven areas in your live where you should establish goals. You will find that each question can be simply answered with a number or a simple yes or no. No stories are necessary—just a number. These questions and others can help you truly evaluate how you are doing in *all* the important areas of your live, including your career. Accurate, honestly tracked numbers do not lie. How you respond to the answers, of course, will be up to you!

"I wish you all the best in accomplishing the needed results to achieve your assigned objectives. Practice the process we reviewed today and add it to your skills of delivering results and keep on delivering results throughout your career."

Reminder Phrases:

Q1: If it's important, you'd better measure it. If you don't, people will not perceive it as important.

Q2: Do what you can, do the best you can, rest very little (Jim Rohn).

Q3: You were created for accomplishment. You are engineered for success (Zig Ziglar).

Q4: Success seems to be connected with action (Conrad Hilton).

Know Your Numbers

Spiritual:

How many times did you attend church last month?

How many days did you say personal prayers last week?

How many times did your family say grace prior to eating last week?

How many times did you help someone last week?

How many times did you read your Bible last week?

How many times did you thank the good Lord for all your blessings today?

Mental:

How many books have you read in the last six months?

How many CD sets did you listen to in your car in the last month?

How many times did you visit the library in the last six months?

How much time did you invest in your personal development last month?

How many times did you really think about what you are thinking about?

Yes/No -Is it what you want to be thinking about?

How many seminars/training/class sessions did you attend last year?

Physical:

How many fruits and vegetables are you eating on average daily?

How much water are you drinking every day?

How many hours of sleep are you getting each night?

How many minutes did you do exercises last week?

What is your resting heart rate?

What is your blood pressure?

What is your cholesterol level?

What is your current weight vs. your target weight?

What is the number of days you missed work in the last year, five years, ten years?

Yes/No—Do you *feel* like a $1,000,000?

Family:

How many meals did you eat together last week?

How many times did you attend church together in the last month?

How many books did you read to your young child last week?

How many times did you help your kids with their homework last week?

How many times a day do you tell your family members you love them?

How many times did you attend your kid's activities (school, sports, music, etc.)?

What was the number of times your family did an event (play in the yard, attend a movie, eat dinner out, walk in the park, etc.) together last month?

How many times did you and your spouse go out on a "date" last month?

How many times did you take a family vacation with all members last year?

Career (if applicable):

What was your last performance rating against your objectives?

What was your last ranking against your peer group?

How many awards/recognitions have you received in the last year?

How many raises did you earn in the last three years?

How many promotions have you earned in the last five years?

How many projects did you volunteer for and complete last year?

How many times did your management come to you for help this quarter?

On what number of key metrics are you above target or below target?

Yes/No—Does your résumé read like someone you would want on your team?

Yes/No –Do you have a differentiator?

School (if applicable):

What are your grades based on your personal goals; the number of A/B/Cs?

What is your ranking in your class or your GPA?

How many hours do you spend studying each day?

How many hours do you have toward your major (if in college)?

How many extracurricular activities do you engage in?

Yes/No—Does your résumé read like someone you would want to hire?

Yes/No -Do you have a differentiator?

Financial:

> Yes/No—Do you have a detailed, written budget?
>
> If yes, how many dollars do you have left at the bottom of your budget after all monthly savings and expenses are accounted for?
>
> What percent of your income do you donate to churches and/or other charities each month?
>
> What percent do you save each month for your college fund (if applicable)?
>
> What percent of your income do you save for retirement?
>
> How much monthly non-house debt do you have in dollars?
>
> How many personal and household expenses did you reduce in the last six months?
>
> How many times have you reviewed and updated your budget this year?

Social Contribution:

> How many times did you drop off unused items at a goodwill-like facility last quarter?
>
> How many hours did you volunteer for something at church, school, neighborhood, town, etc., in the last three months?

Chapter 17

The Final Discussion with My Mentor

When the student is ready, the teacher will appear!

—*Ancient Asian Proverb*

Wow, time really does fly. I met my mentor a short fifteen weeks ago. As we entered the room one last time, I asked Kenneth if he would be willing to listen to a summary of the notes I took during our coaching sessions. He replied, "Of course, and in fact it would be a great way to conclude our mentoring sessions."

I began my overview by stating that Kenneth had shared a tool he had learned from Benjamin Franklin and used for personal development. The concept is to select thirteen skills one wants to develop and improve and focus on each skill one week at a time for thirteen weeks and repeat that process four times each year. "You stated that you could use this process on any list of skills but that you had thirteen you recommend I focus on to start with. Additionally, throughout our sessions, you reinforced that with each skill you would only provide a limited amount of information, research, and experiences and that it was my responsibility to do my own additional research to enhance my knowledge and understanding of each skill. You shared that Mr. Franklin's weekly process provides a methodical way of engraining new skills into one's behavior. But some of these skills can be practiced informally and more frequently if you wish. The key is to focus on them regularly, making them part of your personal philosophy and ultimately your daily habits.

"I understand and see how the process as well as the ongoing homework will enhance my skills and career. In addition to Mr. Franklin's process, you also provided me with thirteen skills you feel are critical to being truly successful in business. I appreciated that your list was not only focused on how to help the company I work for but also composed of many key skills that will help me be successful and have good balance in all areas in my life. I agree that this pursuit of balance will be vital to my total and overall happiness in life.

"The skills you shared with me and challenged me to study, research, and practice are as follows:

1) Always putting the *customer first and being dedicated to serving them* to the best of my abilities

2) Always being *honest* and doing business with only the highest level of *integrity*

3) Establish and write down my specific short-term and long-term *career goals*

4) *Be positive* and *having optimism* even with the most aggressive objectives as they can be achieved with focused concentration and work

5) Learning to balance and *optimize* both the *quality* of the work I do and the *quantity* of the work I do

6) Achieving a high level of business success only comes to individuals who are willing to consistently *go the extra mile*, consistently doing more than they are paid to do

7) Though we focused on skills to enhance my career, remembering that everyone must *have balance in their lives*. You recommended having goals across a minimum of seven important areas in my life (spiritual, mental growth, physical health, family, career, financial, and social contribution)

8) Complementing the seventh skill of a balanced lifestyle, *practicing time management* to help me achieve balance

9) Consistently practicing the skill of *persistence*, a must for long-term success

10) *Working with others* in the many interactions we have in the business world

11) *Learning* something new every day and throughout one's life

12) Saying and living the *Serenity Prayer* for those rocky roads that will occur

13) Lastly, realizing that *results* are the true measure of success in all areas of our lives but especially in business; *numbers* from our measurements really do tell the entire story of what we have accomplished

"These are the thirteen skills you shared with me, and as I have thought about and reflected on them during our time together, I do agree that they are an excellent list of skills that if worked on and mastered over time will truly enhance my career and my success in business and in life. I really appreciate the time, energy, wisdom, and experience you shared with me. I have learned a wealth of information from you. I know this will provide me with a solid foundation for my personal growth. Again, Kenneth, thank you very, very much."

"Cameron, you are very welcome; it was my pleasure. I know what I shared with you along with your focused concentration on each of these thirteen skills will not only bring more value to your customers and drive better business results for the company but also significantly enhance your career and personal life.

"I will leave you with one last philosophy to always remember Cameron. I have had many years of personal experience in the area of negotiations. In this area, one needs to always develop a negotiation strategy prior to entering the discussions. Regardless of the situation or the particular subject being negotiated, there was one philosophy that was used consistently in every strategy. That philosophy was to 'never leave anything on the table.' Though we tried to have an equitable deal for both parties, we worked hard not to leave anything on the table regarding the targeted benefits for our company. I challenge you, as you pursue success and happiness both in your career and in life, to 'never leave anything on the table.' Put your whole heart, soul and all your energy into what you do and enjoy all the dividends you will earn as a result. You are a talented young man; I wish you only the very best. God bless."

Quick Order Form

Telephone Order: 512-944-2435

E-mail Order: goalcoach@verizon.net

Postal Order: Personal Performance Coaching

509 Riverview Drive

Georgetown, Texas 78628

Please send me _____ copies of **The Coach: 13 Skills to Enhance Your Career** in paperback/in hardcover (circle one) at the current retail selling price of each plus sales tax. I understand that I may return them for a full refund for any reason, no questions asked.

Name: _____

Address: _____

City: _____

State: _____

Zip: _____

Telephone: _____

E-mail Address: _____

Please include shipping cost:

- US—$3.00 each
- International—$9.00 each

About the Author

At eighteen years of age, David G. Giese was introduced to his first book on the subject of personal development and the concept that you do not have to be sick to get better. After only studying the topic for a short time, the Author put the basic concepts into practice while earning his college degree. Though only an average student in high school and challenged with a learning disability, David graduated from college in four years with Magna Cum Laude honors and as his business school's top management student.

His professional, high-tech career includes seventeen years at IBM and thirteen years at Dell in many roles including middle management. Throughout his twenty-five years of leadership, he had the opportunity to mentor members of his own work teams and many other colleagues.

The Author is a loving husband of thirty years, a father of two sons, and a picture of health, participating in sprint triathlons annually. David became a certified life coach in 2006 and authored his first book on life skills in 2009. He has positioned himself to pursue his passion of helping others achieve balance in their lives by setting and reaching their goals through the development and practice of important life skills.

CPSIA information can be obtained at www.ICGtesting.com
Printed in the USA
LVOW100457210312

274005LV00002B/11/P